The Scripture in 42 Parables

AND OTHER BUDDHIST CLASSICS FROM THE CHINESE TRANSMISSION

Translated by
Chris Wen-chao Li

MAISON 174
SAN FRANCISCO

Copyright © 2014 Chris Wen-chao Li

Publisher's Cataloging-in-Publication data

Li, Chris Wen-chao:
    The scripture in forty-two parables, and other buddhist classics from the Chinese transmission / translated by Chris Wen-chao Li.
    p. cm.

ISBN:1500627984
ISBN-13:9781500627980

1. Zen Buddhism—Early works to 1800. 2. Tripitaka. Sūtrapitaka. I. Li, Chris Wen-chao, 1968– II. Li, Wen-chao, 1968– III. Title.

Published by:

ꟽ
MAISON 174
174 Stratford Drive
San Francisco, CA 94132
United States of America
maison174@yahoo.com

For Richelle M. Shum and Corey R. Li.

CONTENTS

FOREWORD

By FREDERIK H. GREEN

The origin myth of *The Scripture in 42 Parables*, is, in essence, a tale of translation. Moved by the dream of a flying spirit that was said to portend the enlightened Buddha, emperor Ming-Ti of the Han (58-75 C.E.) dispatched a group of twelve envoys to Scythia who returned with a copy of *The Scripture in 42 Parables*. The scripture was then stored in a temple, and subsequently, as we are told in the pages of Chris Li's masterful translation, "word of the new faith spread far and wide." Omitted from this beautiful fable is an account of the undoubtedly herculean task of the translators who, some two millennia ago, rendered the original text into Chinese and thus made it possible for the source text and the religious teachings contained therein to *spread far and wide*. Indeed, so masterfully did the translators of early Buddhist texts into Chinese perform their task that Buddhism's journey east from what is now northern India did not stop in China, but eventually reached every corner of East Asia. While the names of the Chinese translators of *The Scripture in 42 Parables* or *The Eight Understandings from the Realm of Higher Beings* are unknown or of questionable origin, the translation of *The Heart of the Virtue of Wisdom*, the third of the texts contained in this volume, is typically attributed to the famous monk Hsuan Tsang (602-664), whose epic journey to India in search of sacred Buddhist texts has been retold in the Chinese novel *Journey to the West*. Yet regardless of whether their names are known, it is thanks to their linguistic prowess and their belief both in the translatability of the texts and the value of the religious teachings contained therein that these early translators succeeded in their task and thus not only contributed to the spread of Buddhism, but also insured the afterlife of the original Sanskrit texts, many of which have since been lost, in places and times far removed from the events described in the original sutras.

How did these translators achieve that these sutras, the complexity of which was not only of lexical and syntactical nature, but more importantly of semantic and hermeneutical dimension, were accepted by Chinese readers? In the case of *The Scripture in 42 Parables*, the intrinsic foreignness of the original, it appears, was mitigated by the deliberate use of Chinese stylistic features. Robert Sharf believes that the phrase "fo yen" for example, that is used to introduce most sections and that is rendered in the translation at hand as "says the Buddha" is reminiscent of the use of the phrase "the master said" in *The Analects* (Lunyü)[1]. The use of the word "tao," a key concept both of Chinese Taoism and Confucianism, to render not only the term mārga, or noble path to enlightenment, but also terms like nirvāna or dharma, is another example of this practice that can be observed in *The Scripture in 42 Parables*. Early Chinese translations, as we can see, are not merely word-for-word renderings of Indic texts, but attempts at making

---

[1] Sharf, Robert H. "The Scripture in Forty-two Sections," in Donald S. Lopez (ed.), *Religions of China In Practice*. Princeton: Princeton University Press, 1996, pp. 360-364.

tangible the very elusive nature of foreign philosophical-religious concepts by cloaking these complex foreign terms in existing terminology and concepts. While later translations might have been more discriminative — dharma, for example, is at times phonetically rendered as "tamo" (達摩) or semantically as "fa" (法) – the foremost concern of the translators of *The Scripture in 42 Parables* and other early texts, it seems, was to gain wide acceptance and popularity of the religious teachings of Buddhism. They thus chose a strategy that is typically regarded as domestication, a process whereby complex cultural or linguistic concepts are expressed through translations that attempt to facilitate the reading of the original by using a style and word choice that is easily recognizable to the target audience.

Domestication is also the most outstanding feature of the translations by Chris Li collected in this volume. Treating the source text as a literary and cultural text that will provide readers with a better understanding of what Buddhism has come to mean in its larger cultural context of East Asia rather than as a religious doctrine the careful study of which will provide clear guidance to professional practitioners, Li is above all concerned with comprehensibility. While his translations are masterful in both their accuracy and readability, they are not meant to complement an existing body of technical translations that explore the doctrinal or hermeneutical particulars of existing sutras. Li does not expect his readers to be overly familiar with the cultural-historical context in which these works were produced or read, nor does he provide such context in the form of excessive footnotes. Instead, Li wants his readers to enjoy their reading experience and to intuitively take in some of the beauty and spiritual quality inherent in the original. No doubt, he succeeds on both counts.

If success of the early Chinese translations of Buddhist texts rested on their translators' linguistic prowess as well as intimate familiarity with multiple socio-cultural environments, Li's translations are likewise destined to replicate their success. Trained as a linguist and interpreter, Li has distinguished himself not only as an accomplished scholar and teacher, but also as a widely published practitioner of the art of translation. Furthermore, as a multi-lingual and bi-cultural citizen of the world, Li is uniquely positioned to mediate between cultures and to help satisfy the growing interest in Chinese culture in the West. While the concept of domestication guides his approach to translation, Li does not sacrifice accuracy or completeness. Instead, he chooses to flexibly adopt his approach to whatever challenge the source text poses. Where the Chinese can be succinct and extremely compact, as in the last line of the second of the 42 parables where 12 characters suffice in Chinese, Li provides us with 5 lines of text to convey the profundity of the concept of Buddhist enlightenment. The 4th of the 8 understandings, he presents to us in a tone almost reminiscent of biblical commands and it thus seems strangely familiar to readers with a Judeo-Christian cultural background. In passage 38 of the *Heart of the Virtue of Wisdom*, finally, he chooses to speak to us with a vivid directness. "You don't get it," we read when the

Buddha turns to a sramana who misunderstands his words, sensing that instead, by virtue of Li's highly original translation, we might be the ones who *get it*. Li's translation will speak to many audiences. The general reader will be drawn to its accessible prose as much as the specialist who will delight in Li's analytical abilities and profound grasp of classical Chinese. Because it provides both source text and translation, students of Chinese and of translation will marvel at this masterful display of linguistic and cultural transfer. This text, it is hoped, only presents the beginning of a long series of translations of Chinese texts of cultural significance to be published by *Maison 174*.

—FREDERIK H. GREEN. PH.D. is Assistant Professor of Chinese Literature at San Francisco State University

xii

INTRODUCTION

By CHRIS WEN-CHAO LI

Collected in this volume are three of the most widely-disseminated shorter canonical texts of East Asian buddhism, namely *The Scripture in Forty-Two Parables*, *The Eight Revelations from the Realm of Higher Beings*, and *The Heart of the Virtue of Wisdom*, presented in a new domesticated translation based on a literary reading of the Chinese source texts.

The Scripture in Forty-Two Parables (四十二章經, a.k.a. *The Sūtra in Forty-Two Sections*, *The Sūtra in Forty-Two Parts*, or *The Sūtra of Forty-Two Chapters*), dating to A.D. 67, is believed by many to be the earliest work of buddhism to be introduced from India into China, and as such is afforded special status in Chinese buddhism and folklore. The scripture is divided into forty-two sections, consisting for the most part of direct quotes from the Buddha addressing an audience of entry-level initiates. The forty-two sections are short—many under a hundred characters in length—and adopt a format that is significantly different from discourses translated from the Sanskrit in later periods of the Chinese transmission, a format which instead shares similarities with Taoist and Confucian texts of the time, leading some scholars to hypothesize a Chinese or hybrid Chinese–Central Asian origin for the text. In the scripture, explanation of buddhist concepts is done in colloquial language, and vivid metaphors are created to relate core beliefs to such daily concerns as family, marriage, charity, wealth, ambition, temptation, and sex. References to *The Scripture in Forty-Two Parables* appear in such Chinese historical records as the *Annals of the Later Han* (後漢書), and play a central role in the martial arts novel *The Deer and the Cauldron* (鹿鼎記) by cult author Louis Cha (金庸). *The Scripture in Forty-Two Parables* is regarded as one of three canonical legacy teachings of the Buddha (佛遺教三經) in the Zen buddhist traditions of China, Japan and Korea.

The Eight Revelations from the Realm of Higher Beings (八大人覺經, a.k.a., *The.Sūtra of the Eight Realizations of Great Beings* or *The Eight Great Awakenings Sūtra*) is another of the Buddha's three legacy teachings of the East Asian Zen tradition, similarly directed at an audience of initiates and written in the vernacular style characteristic of early buddhist transmissions to China. The exact date of the work's completion is unknown, and the attribution of the translation to the Parthian scholar-translator Lokottama is believed to be of dubious origin. As with *The Scripture in Forty-Two Parables*, the Chinese "translation" is the only extant version of the text. *The Eight Revelations from the Realm of Higher Beings* takes as its subject the impermanence of the psycho-physical world and the illusory nature of sensory experiences, pointing out that attachment and desire lie at the heart of these illusions, and, in the latter half of the scripture, goes on to prescribe methods to see past these illusions. The discourse comprises a mere three hundred seventy-two characters, but is among the most celebrated and most commonly recited texts in the East Asian buddhist tradition.

With a similar emphasis on the illusory nature of reality is the third text in this series, *The Heart of the Virtue of Wisdom*, better known as the *Prajñāpāramitā Heart Sūtra* (般若波羅蜜多心經, *Prajñāpāramitā. Hṛdaya Sūtra*)—

arguably the most revered and most commonly chanted scripture in *all* of the world's buddhist traditions. The sūtra, occupying a mere two hundred sixty characters, is believed to be a condensation (hence the "heart") of the *Mahāprajñāpāramitā* (Greater *Prajñāpāramitā*), a compendium of writings exploring the human virtue known as wisdom, and is attributed to the Indian philosopher Nāgārjuna. In its brief length, the *Heart Sūtra* touches upon virtually all of the core concepts of buddhist philosophy, including the five *skandhas*, the twelve *āyatanas*, the eighteen *dhātus*, and the twelve *nidānas*, along with *dukkha* and the Four Noble Truths, explaining eventually that all such dogmatic teachings, along with the psycho-physical world we live in and the sensory stimuli we experience, are illusory in nature, and must be understood as such before one can move on to a higher level of understanding (*anuttarā samyak-saṃbodhi*) and approach the blissful state of *nirvāṇa*. The sūtra ends atypically with a transliterated *dhāraṇī* mnemonic for chanting, a verse which, in many regional buddhist traditions, is believed to be imbued with spiritual or transcendental powers.

Though recorded in history as having been translated from Sanskrit into Classical Chinese, recent scholarship[2] is of the view that the *Heart Sūtra* is more likely of Chinese origin in the light of grammatical and stylistic peculiarities in the Sanskrit *Heart Sūtra* suggesting that it was not an original work but rather a translation from the Chinese, and that the original Chinese *Heart Sūtra* was most likely cobbled together from longer Chinese

---

[2] See Nattier, Jan. 1992. "The Heart Sūtra: A Chinese Apocryphal Text?". *Journal of the Internation Association of Buddhist Studies* 15 (2): 153-223.

texts such as the *Dharmapada*, which can be verifiably traced to extant Sanskrit sources. The *Heart Sūtra* currently exists in multiple recensions in Chinese, Tibetan, and South Asian languages, with the earliest extant Chinese version purportedly dating to the fifth century C.E. The source text on which we base the current translation however is the seventh century translation of Tang dynasty scholar-monk Hsuan Tsang (602-664), widely seen as the most authoritative and currently the most widely disseminated version in the East Asian tradition. Hsuan Tsang's translation is an instance of the shorter variant of the *Heart Sūtra*, believed to be of greater antiquity; there exists another longer variant that begins with a description of the setting at which the sermon was preached ("Thus have I heard. The Lord was preaching at..."), and ends with the audience reaction to the teachings thus transmitted, bringing the format in line with that of standard Mahāyāna scripture.

The method of translation adopted this volume differs somewhat from that found in most existing buddhist translations into English. In this collection, the Chinese originals are treated as literary in nature, and a structuralist reading is applied to arrive at the meaning of the text. A domesticating strategy is then used to render the cultural elements of the narrative in an attempt to create dynamic equivalence between the experiences of source and target language audiences.

Most buddhist sūtra translations cater to an audience of religious devotees, and aim to present the text within a larger doctrinal framework, thereby making it necessary to adopt technical terminology, most of it in transliterated form, consistent with a wider body of literature and scholarly works on the subject. To a lesser extent, translating with a religious purpose often means that the wording of the original source text is treated as sacred, creating less incentive to make adjustments in diction, imagery, word order, and cultural expectations that would allow the text to read more naturally to a target language audience. Furthermore there is a reluctance on the part of some translators to draw from the large reservoir of religious terms in the English language for fear that Judeo-Christian connotations would distort the reader's understanding of buddhism. The cumulative effect of these translation practices is that, to the uninitiated reader, buddhist literature in the English language cannot be understood on its own, but requires footnotes laden with background information to supplement the already dense and impenetrable lines of jargon and foreignisms— which is far from the experience of the original audience of devotees listening to the Buddha preach his message. That is to say, whereas the original consisted of readily comprehensible spoken discourse, most translations into English end up as treatises meant to be studied rather than read.

In this volume, the Chinese originals are treated as literary rather than sacred texts, and steps are taken to produce equivalent literary effect in the experience of the English language reader. This includes the borrowing of religious notions most familiar to readers of an Anglo-American cultural background and adjustments in collocation and word order so as to preserve the idiomaticity and propositional logic of the original. A structuralist reading is adopted in the interpretation of the source texts in that meaning is not based on the teachings of a particular master or the traditions of a particular sect or lineage, but rather is reached through an examination of relations between lexical elements of the text itself that contribute to propositional meaning. Where imagery and metaphor is concerned, a domesticating strategy is adopted which seeks dynamic rather than formal equivalence, using cultural translation to render examples comprehensible—for what is familiar and prosaic in one culture may not be so in another: "lamb of God" and "daily bread" are familiar images from the Judeo-Christian bible which assume a familiarity with sheep husbandry and the consumption of bread as a daily staple, both of which may come across as exotic in a culture absent bread and sheep, in which case the replacement of bread with, say, rice, and sheep with local livestock may be appropriate in translation. We do the same when we replace the Chinese musical instrument *qin* with the fiddle to remove unwanted exoticness that distracts from the main message of the discourse.

The ultimate purpose of this approach to translation is to maximize comprehensibility upon initial reading, so that the reader without background can get a general sense of the message instantaneously, much like how the viewer of a comedy sitcom can get the jokes right away, rather than having to resort to footnotes to explain why a joke is supposed to be funny. There is, of course, a price to pay for this immediacy, which is that much of the cultural background and religious specificity of the source text may be lost in the rush to arrive at the gist of the message. To this criticism, we emphasize that the current text is not intended to replace existing scholarly translations, but rather to supplement them, with the understanding that no one translation can be an exact replica of the original, and that, much like no single photograph can fully represent a three-dimensional object, a multitude of different translations is needed to achieve a fuller understanding of the source text. To quote the Elizabethan translator John Dolman[3],

> Knowing that if such as have greater knowledge to set forth things more exactly should hear my plainness not overmuch discommended, they then should be more provoked with hope of the marvelous fame that their doings should deserve if they listed to employ some pains in attempting the like.

In a way, the current translation is designed to fill a niche, and by targeting the non-buddhist general public the hope is that a greater understanding and appreciation will be gained for these literary artifacts of Mahayana buddhism propagated via the Chinese transmission.

—CHRIS WEN-CHAO LI. D. PHIL., is Professor of Chinese Linguistics at San Francisco State University

---

[3] Preface to the *Tusculan Questions* (1561).

四十二章經

後漢迦葉摩騰、竺法蘭同譯

Chris Wen-chao Li

The Scripture in
42 Parables

Translated from the Chinese of Gobharana
and Kasyapa Matanga

昔漢孝明皇帝夜夢見神人，身體有金色，項有日光，飛在殿前，意中訢然，甚悅之。

明日問臣：此為何神也？有通人傅毅曰：臣聞天竺有得道者，號曰佛，輕舉能飛，殆將其神也。

於是上悟，即遣使者張騫、羽林中郎將秦景博士弟子王遵等十二人，至大月支國寫取佛經四十章。

在第十四石函中登起立塔寺，於是道法流布，處處修立佛寺。遠人伏化願為臣妾者，不可稱數，國內清寧，含識之類蒙恩受賴，於今不絕也。

PREAMBLE

There appeared in the dream of Han dynasty emperor Ming-Ti a holy apparition: a heavenly form with a torso of gold and a collar of bright luminescence—the picture of celestial bliss—flying into the imperial court.

Moved by this vision, the emperor inquired of his subjects what this omen might portend, to which the accomplished and worldly-wise Fu-Yi replied, "In the kingdom of the Hindus there is a holy one by the name of Buddha who is said to have arrived at enlightenment and can fly at will—he perhaps is the seraph in your dream."

Having understood the premonition, the emperor dispatched a delegation of twelve royal academicians led by Chang Ch'ien, Ch'in Ching and Wang Tsun to the realm of Gatae, from which they brought back *The Scripture in 42 Parables.*

The scripture was stored in the fourteenth stone vault of Lan-tai, at which location a sacred tower was erected. Word of the new faith spread far and wide. Temples were built throughout the kingdom and worshippers poured in from distant corners. Peace was upon the land, and those able to appreciate the transformation are reaping its benefits to this day.

世尊成道已，作是思惟：

　　離欲寂靜，是最為勝；
　　住大禪定，降諸魔道。

於鹿野苑中轉四諦法輪，度憍陳如等
五人，而證道果。復有比丘所說諸疑
，求佛進止。世尊教敕，一一開悟。
合掌敬諾。而順世尊敕。

PROLOGUE

Upon attaining enlightenment, he who will forever be honored by this world had the following thoughts to share with his fellow man:

True deliverance you will find
When you cease to become a slave to desire,
For your inner demons can scarce conspire
In this fully awakened state of mind.

In the Royal Deer Park, the four noble truths[1] were preached to Kaundinya and others—a total of five disciples who eventually gained entry into the enlightened realm. Other Bhiksus came forth in search of answers, to which the Buddha complied and explained in detail. The Bhiksus folded their palms in gratitude and were converted to the faith.

---

[1] The four noble truths being (1) that life consists of suffering, (2) that suffering is brought about by desire; (3) that an end to suffering is within reach, and (4) that the path to ending suffering lies with achieving full mindfulness.

佛言：辭親出家，識心達本，解無有法，名曰沙門。常行二百五十戒，進止清淨，為四真道行，成阿羅漢。

阿羅漢者，能飛行變化，曠劫壽命，住動天地。

次為阿那含。阿那含者，壽終靈神，上十九天，證阿羅漢。

次為斯陀含。斯陀含者，一上一還，即得阿羅漢。

次為須陀洹。須陀洹者，七死七生，便證阿羅漢。

愛欲斷者，如四肢斷，不復用之。

(1) Life as a Sramana

Says the Buddha:

Sramanas[2] are those who leave behind their families to join the monastic life in search of higher teachings to see into the nature of the mind.

Sramanas live life pure and simple, guided by 250 buddhist precepts. They work their way through the four stages of achievement on the path to becoming an *arhat*.

An arhat[3] is one who can fly in the air and alter his physical appearance; he has a lifespan of eons, and is attuned to the vibrations of heaven and earth.

A step below the arhat is the *anagamin*[4]. Anagamins ascend to the 19th level of heaven upon the end of their human existence, and graduate to arhathood.

A step below the anagamin is the *sakridagamin*. Sakridagamins are a lifetime away from becoming arhats.

Below the sakridagamin is the *srotapanna*, who has yet to go through 7 rounds of rebirth before reaching the stage of arhat.

---

[2] Monks, nuns, and other monastics.

[3] A saint or immortal—one who has achieved perfection.

[4] One who has been liberated from the cycle of death and rebirth.

佛言：出家沙門者，斷欲去愛，識自心源，達佛深理，悟無為法。

內無所得，外無所求；心不繫道，亦不結業，無念無作，非修非證。

不歷諸位，而自崇最，名之為道。

As a sramana, once you have cut yourself loose from all emotion and desire, it is like amputating your limbs—once the cut is made, expect never to use them again.

(2) An End to All Desire

Says the Buddha:

As a sramana who has renounced the worldly life, you must do away with all emotion and desire so as to tap into your true nature. Then you will relate to the teachings of the Buddha and appreciate the profound wisdom within.

You will arrive at a state where you need cling to nothing from within, and seek nothing from without.

You will form no attachments to any specific teachings, and in so doing, incur no negative karma.

Should you find yourself blank in thought and inert in action, practicing no precepts and producing no work, then, behold, you have arrived at the highest level, without having to clear the intermediate stages—this is what enlightenment is all about.

佛言：剃除鬚髮而為沙門。受道法者，去世資財，乞求取足。日中一食，樹下一宿，慎勿再矣。使人愚蔽者，愛與欲也。

(3) Giving up Worldly Goods

Says the Buddha:

You should shave your head to join the order. In line with our teachings, you agree to give up all your worldly belongings and live life by begging for the bare essentials. At noon, you will eat your only meal of the day, and at night, sleep in the shade of a tree. You will ask for no more than this, for desire and attachment can cloud one's perception.

佛言：眾生以十事為善，亦以十事為
惡。何等為十？身三、口四、意三。
身三者：殺、盜、婬。口四者：兩舌
、惡口、妄言、綺語。意三者：嫉、
恚、癡。如是十事，不順聖道，名十
惡行。是惡若止，名十善行耳。

(4) Understanding Good and Evil

Says the Buddha:

Good comes in ten forms, and evil comes in ten forms. What are the ten forms of evil, you ask? Of the ten, three are evils of the body, four are evils of speech, and another three are evils of the mind. The three evils of the body are killing, stealing and lustfulness. The four evils of speech are rumor-mongering, slander, fabrication, and flattery. The three evils of mind are envy, rage, and self-deceit. The ten evils are so named because they hinder one's progress to sainthood. Should you be able to stay away from the ten evils, then you have in you the ten forms of good.

佛言：人有眾過而不自悔頓息其心，罪來赴身，如水歸海，漸成深廣。若人有過，自解知非，改惡行善，罪自消滅；如病得汗，漸有痊損耳。

(5) Walk Away from Sin

Says the Buddha:

Should you sin and not repent, the moment of retribution will be upon you in a flash. The negativity will slowly add up, and, like water flowing towards the sea, the cumulative effect will be vast beyond imagination. Whereas if you repent your sins and change for the better, the negativity would wear off, much like how sweating in the course of an illness leads to full recovery.

佛言：惡人聞善，故來擾亂者，汝自
禁息，當無瞋責。彼來惡者，而自惡
之。

(6) Maintaining Calm in the Face of Evil

Says the Buddha:

There are those who cannot stand the thought of someone doing good, and will do everything in their power to get in your way. At this point, do not lash out, but instead, keep your calm, for what goes around comes around—evil, in the end, will always be revisited upon the evildoer.

佛言：有人聞吾守道，行大仁慈，故致罵佛。佛默不對。罵止，問曰：子以禮從人，其人不納，禮歸子乎？對曰：歸矣。佛言：今子罵我，我今不納，子自持禍，歸子身矣。猶響應聲，影之隨形，終無免離。慎勿為惡！

(7) What Goes Around Comes Around

Says the Buddha:

There was a man who, upon hearing that I, the Buddha, was practicing compassion and benevolence, took it upon himself to provoke me by unleashing a barrage of insults. To these insults I said nothing. When the insults ended, I asked:

"What happens when you give somebody a present and they refuse it?"

"The gift stays with you."

"So what do you think happens when you hurl insults at me, and I refuse your insults? The insults stay with you. The negativity is visited upon yourself."

This much is certain: for every noise, an echo follows; for every form, a shadow follows; for every act of evil, retribution isn't far behind. So steer clear of evil.

佛言：惡人害賢者，猶仰天而唾。唾不至天，還從己墮。逆風揚塵，塵不至彼，還坌己身。賢不可毀，禍必滅己。

(8) Spitting at the Sky

Says the Buddha:

When an evildoer tries to do harm to a good person, it is like trying to spit at the sky—the spit will eventually come down and drop on the spitter.

Or you can also say it is like throwing sand at the wind—the wind will turn it back, and the sand will rain down on you, soiling your clothes.

So the moral is, the good cannot be maligned—those who try to malign them will only bring harm to themselves.

佛言：博聞愛道，道必難會。守志奉
道，其道甚大。

(9) Be True to Your Heart

Says the Buddha:

Those who claim a love for the truth and actively seek it out seldom find what they are looking for. Instead, truth resides in those who have faith, and is fostered by the people who live by it.

佛言：睹人施道，助之歡善，得福甚大。沙門問曰：此福盡乎？佛言：譬如一炬之火，數千百人，各以炬來分取，熟食除冥。此炬如故，福亦如之。

(10) More Blessed to Give Than to Receive

Says the Buddha:

Are you the type to happily join in when the word is preached to the masses? If so, you are blessed with divine grace.

A sramana asks:

What if this grace is stretched to the limit? Won't the blessings run out?

Says the Buddha

Let's say you have a torch, and with this torch you help a thousand others light their fires, so they can cook and be warm. Now does your own flame grow weaker because you extended it and shared it with people? Not so with fires, and not so with blessings either.

佛言：

飯惡人百，不如飯一善人；

飯善人千，不如飯一持五戒者；

飯五戒者萬，不如飯一須陀洹；

飯百萬須陀洹，不如飯一斯陀含；

飯千萬斯陀含，不如飯一阿那含；

飯一億阿那含，不如飯一阿羅漢；

飯十億阿羅漢，不如飯一辟支佛；

飯百億辟支佛，不如飯一三世諸佛；

飯千億三世諸佛，不如飯一

無念無住無修無證之者。

(11) Expressions of Charity

Says the Buddha:

Feeding a hundred crooks
  cannot compare to feeding one honest civilian;
Feeding a thousand civilians
  cannot compare to feeding one avowed ascetic;
Feeding a million ascetics
  cannot compare to feeding one certified *srotapanna*;
Feeding a billion *srotapannas*
  cannot compare to feeding one accomplished
    sakridagamin;
Feeding a trillion *sakridagamins*
  cannot compare to feeding one heavenly *anagamin*;
Feeding a quadrillion *anagamins*
  cannot compare to feeding one enlightened *arhat*;
Feeding a quintillion *arhats*
  cannot compare to feeding one *Pratyeka Buddha*;
Feeding a sextillion *Pratyeka Buddhas*
  cannot compare to feeding one *Triloka Buddha*;
Feeding a septillion *Triloka Buddhas*
  cannot compare to feeding one who is beyond it all,
    who conceives of nothing and is attached to
      nothing, who practices nothing and produces
        nothing.

佛言：人有二十難：
貧窮布施難、豪貴學道難；
棄命必死難、得睹佛經難；
生值佛世難、忍色忍欲難；
見好不求難、被辱不瞋難；
有劫不臨難、觸事無心難；
廣學博究難、除滅我慢難；
不輕末學難、心行平等難；
不說是非難、會善知識難；
見性學道難、隨化度人難；
睹境不動難、善解方便難。

(12) Life is Hard

Says the Buddha:

Life is fraught with challenges; here are twenty such tests of your resolve:

— To give to charity when you are poor,
— To be pious in faith when you are rich;

— To show bravery in the face of imminent danger,
— To remain unenticed by pleasures of the flesh;

— To be born in the age of spiritual teachings,
— To bear witness to the propagation of the word;

— To not want what is desirable to all,
— To not abuse the power in hand;

— To not rile over unsettling change,
— To not lash out when put to shame;

— To not judge the rights and wrongs of others,
— To treat every person as one and the same;

— To not despise those less enlightened,
— To not indulge the ego within;

— To appreciate learning for all its richness,
— To have peers to share in learned pursuit;

— To know thyself and seek to better it,
— To lend assistance to your fellow man;

— To not be roused by fleeting sentiment,
— To see pathways to enlightenment for what they are.

沙門問佛：以何因緣，得知宿命，會其至道？

佛言：淨心守志，可會至道。譬如磨鏡，垢去明存。斷欲無求，當得宿命。

(13) Understanding Destiny

A sramana asks:

What does it take to know one's destiny and understand the workings of fate?

Says the Buddha:

Determination and clarity of mind are what you need to arrive at total understanding. Much like when you clean a mirror, once the grime is removed, you begin to see your true reflection. So it is with the pursuit of understanding: once desire and greed are washed away, your destiny will reveal itself.

沙門問佛：何者為善？何者最大？

佛言：行道守真者善，志與道合者大
。

(14) The Greatest Good

A sramana asks:

What does it mean to be good?
What is the greatest good?

Says the Buddha:

Good is when you can take the high road without fear of turning into a hypocrite. When your heart and your morals are one, the greatest good is within you.

沙門問佛：何者多力？何者最明？

佛言：忍辱多力，不懷惡故，兼加安健。忍者無惡，必為人尊。

心垢滅盡，淨無暇穢，是為最明。未有天地，逮於今日，十方所有，無有不見，無有不知，無有不聞。得一切智，可謂明矣。

(15) Power and Brilliance

A sramana asks:

What human ability is the most powerful?
What personal quality shines brightest?

Says the Buddha:

When you can take humiliation and not hold a
grudge, it is a sign of your self-assurance and poise,
and there can be no greater power, for genuine
humility earns you respect.

What shines brightest is the mind, rid of its
impurities and restored to its pristine state. For then
you will see all there is to see, hear all there is to hear,
and know all there is to know. Knowing all, you will
possess knowledge from all corners, from the
beginning of time to the present moment – that is
what it means to be truly stellar.

佛言：大懷愛欲，不見道者，譬如澄水，致手攬之：眾人共臨。無有睹其影者？人以愛欲交錯，心中濁興，故不見道。汝等沙門，當捨愛欲。愛欲垢盡，道可見矣。

(16) Pull Away from Desire

Says the Buddha:

When a man is blinded by desire and cannot see the light, it is like when you reach into a stream and stir up the sediment. Now gaze into the water and what do you see? Certainly not your own reflection. So it is when desire clouds your judgment. So my beloved sramanas, pull away from desire, and you will have wiped the dust off the mirror that will allow you to see the true path.

佛言：夫見道者，譬如持炬，入冥室中，其冥即滅，而明獨存。學道見諦，無明即滅，而明常存矣。

(17) Illuminating Ignorance

Says the Buddha:

When you see the light, it is like when a man holding a torch walks into a dark chamber. The darkness is driven away and only brightness remains. Once you arrive at the truth, ignorance is fended off and eternal understanding prevails.

佛言：吾法念無念念，行無行行，言無言言，修無修修。會者近爾，迷者遠乎。言語道斷，非物所拘。差之毫釐，失之須臾。

(18) The Nature of Things

Says the Buddha:

I teach you to think the unthinkable, do the undoable, speak the unspeakable, and work the unworkable. Those who get it get it, those who don't don't—for all the words in the world cannot describe the sublimity of this truth. Be off by a hair's breadth or miss it by a fraction of a second and the picture is false.

佛言：觀天地，念非常。觀世界，念非常。觀靈覺，即菩提。如是知識，得道疾矣。

(19) False Façades

Says the Buddha:

As you gaze upon heaven and earth, consider their impermanence; as you look down at the world, consider its impermanence; whereas when you stumble upon spiritual awakening, know that you have found the single permanent truth—inquire after knowledge in this manner, and enlightenment will be upon you.

佛言：當今身中四大，各自有名。都
無我者，我既都無，其如幻耳。

(20) All is Immaterial

Says the Buddha:

We say that the body is made up of the four elements, and we give each of these elements a name. But to each name is there a substance to match? Is there substance to each of the names? Or are they tricks of the mind?

佛言：人隨情欲，求於聲名。聲名顯著，身已故矣。

貪世常名，而不學道，枉功勞形。

譬如燒香：雖人聞香，香之燼矣。危身之火，而在其後。

(21) Seeking Recognition

Says the Buddha:

Born with the instinct, we are urged on to seek fame and recognition. Yet when fame and recognition are finally ours, there is precious little time left to enjoy the fruits of our labor.

So those who are trapped in the rat race and devote little time to matters of faith are, to say the least, letting their lives waste away.

Liken it to burning a stick of incense – what fragrance it gives off is at the cost of the destruction of its core. Sooner or later the fire will consume it whole.

佛言：財色於人，人之不捨，譬如刀
刃有蜜，不足一餐之美。小兒舐之，
則有割舌之患。

(22) Money and Sex

Says the Buddha:

The temptation of money and sex, for most people, is like that of a sharp knife coated with honey: sweet, but not worth the trouble. A little kid who doesn't know better might be tempted to lick the knife, but just watch him cut his tongue!

佛言：人繫於妻子舍宅，甚於牢獄。
牢獄有散釋之期，妻子無遠離之念。

情愛於色，豈憚驅馳？雖有虎口之患
，心存甘伏，投泥自溺，故曰凡夫。

透得此門，出塵羅漢。

(23) Ball and Chain

Says the Buddha:

The bind of wife, children, and home is more suffocating than the bars of a prison cell. With prison, at least you're free to go when you've served your term. But with a wife, there is no end to the bondage.

Such emotional attachments are really only based on lust, so why not just walk away?

Ordinary people however are all too willing to fall for this ruse; they know they're going to be swallowed whole, yet they willingly walk towards the she-wolf's open jaws.

The few who are able to sidestep this trap and keep their freedom intact stand a better chance of becoming *arhats*.

佛言：愛欲莫甚於色。色之為欲，其大無外。

賴有一矣。若使二同，普天之人，無能為道者矣。

(24) Obsessed with Sex

Says the Buddha:

As temptations go, there is no greater force than sex. Who can resist the lure of sexual attraction?

Be grateful there is only one such temptation dangling before our eyes—were we to be presented with a second, who in this world would ever make it to the enlightened realm?

佛言：愛欲之人，猶如執炬，逆風而行，必有燒手之患。

(25) Burned by Lust

Says the Buddha:

A man driven by lust is like a hand carrying a torch against the force of the wind. Sooner or later, he is going to burn himself.

天神獻玉女於佛，欲壞佛意。佛言：
革囊眾穢，爾來何為？去！吾不用。

天神愈敬，因問道意。佛為解說，即
得須陀洹果。

(26) Tale of Temptation

When the Buddha was nearing enlightenment, the gods sent to earth a luscious virgin to test his resolve, whereupon the Buddha said to the virgin, "Get lost, you dirtbag! What are you doing here? Go back to where you belong! I have no use for you."

With this he earned the full respect of the gods, who inquired of him the path to sainthood, and as he explained, he was magically transformed into a *srotapanna*.

佛言：夫為道者，猶木在水：尋流而行，不觸兩岸。不為人取，不為鬼神所遮，不為洄流所住，亦不腐敗，吾保此木，決定入海。

學道之人，不為情欲所惑，不為眾邪所嬈，精進無為，吾保此人，必得道矣。

(27) Staying the Course

A seeker of the truth is like flotsam drifting out to sea. As it floats downstream, the journey is fraught with variables: it may wash ashore, or rot might set in, or currents may cause it to sink, or a passer-by might pick it up, or evil spirits may snatch it away. If it clears all of the above hurdles, then to be sure, the wood is destined for ocean waters.

Similar hurdles await those on the path to spiritual progress: emotions clouding reason, the temptation of the illicit... If one could only stay focused, I guarantee, enlightenment is not far off.

佛言：慎勿信汝意，汝意不可信。慎勿與色會，色會即禍生。得阿羅漢已，乃可信汝意。

(28) Primal Instincts

Says the Buddha:

Don't trust your gut feelings – your feelings are unreliable. Don't give in to sex – sex will do you in. Only when you've become an *arhat* can you begin to go with your instincts.

佛言：慎勿視女色，亦莫共言語。若與語者，正心思念。我為沙門，處於濁世，當如蓮華，不為泥汙。想其老者如母，長者如姊，少者如妹，稚者如子。生度脫心，息滅惡念。

(29) The Fairer Sex

Says the Buddha:

Don't look at women, don't talk to women. If you have to talk to them, detach yourself and be reminded that you are an avowed *sramana* striving to stay pure in a filthy world, like a lotus rising out of the mud.

As you face her, if she is advanced in years, look on her as your mother; if she is more mature than you, treat her like your big sister; if she is younger than you, think of your younger siblings; if she is underage, regard her as your daughter. Banish all impure thoughts and work towards the greater good.

佛言：夫為道者，如被乾草，火來須避。道人見欲，必當遠之。

(30) Avoiding Temptation

If you're in the business of making hay, come fire season, you move your hay. If spiritual progress is your calling, come temptation, you know to get out of its way.

佛言：有人患淫不止，欲自斷陰。

佛謂之曰：若斷其陰，不如斷心。心如功曹：功曹若止，從者都息。邪心不止，斷陰何益？

佛為說偈：

欲生於汝意，
意以思想生；
二心各寂靜，
非色亦非行。

佛言，此偈是迦葉佛說。

(31) Cure for a Lonely Heart

There lived a man who was slave to his sexual urges and was seriously contemplating severing his masculine member, to which the Buddha remarked:

What good is cutting off the penis? It's your mind that needs to be shut off. The mind is the motor, you see. Once the motor is turned down, the machine will no longer spew dirty thoughts,

At which point the Buddha burst into verse:

> *Desires take shape as passing thoughts,*
> *Thoughts are born of a wandering mind;*
> *Stilling thought and mind should move the heart*
> *To leave urges and delusions behind.*

The words of Kasyapa Buddha, he said.

佛言：人從愛欲生憂，從憂生怖。若
離於愛，何憂何怖？

(32) Letting Go

Says the Buddha:

Desire brings about anxiety, anxiety brings about fear.
Let go of all desire, and it will dawn on you: What is
there to be anxious about? What is there to fear?

佛言：夫為道者，譬如一人與萬人戰。挂鎧出門，意或怯弱，或半路而退，或格鬥而死，或得勝而還。

沙門學道，應當堅持其心：精進勇銳，不畏前境，破滅眾魔，而得道果。

(33) Battling Your Inner Demons

Going down the spiritual path is like battling millions with an army of one. As you march out in full gear, fear starts to set in. You may choose to quit halfway. Or you may fall in the line of duty. Or you may eventually make it back a hero.

So it is with spiritual pursuits. Like in battle, you must show courage and resolve as you take apart the enemy's defenses – and once you do, the spoils of war are yours for the taking.

沙門夜誦迦葉佛遺教經，其聲悲緊，思悔欲退。

佛問之曰：汝昔在家，曾為何業？

對曰：愛彈琴。

佛言：弦緩如何？

對曰：不鳴矣。

弦急如何？

對曰：聲絕矣。

急緩得中如何？

對曰：諸音普矣。

(34) Finding Your Pace

The Buddha chanced upon a sramana reciting the *Teachings of Kaspaya Buddha* late into the night, in a voice that was at once sad and tense. The sramana was on the verge of abandoning the calling when the Buddha asked,

"Tell me, before you joined the order, what did you do for a living?"

"I was a fiddler."

"Now when you play the fiddle, what happens if the strings are too loose?"

"No sound comes forth."

"And if they are strung too tight?"

"The instrument screeches like mad."

"What about when they're tuned just right?"

"Then you get music."

佛言：沙門學道亦然。心若調適，道可得矣。於道若暴，暴即身疲；其身若疲，意即生惱；意若生惱，行即退矣。其行既退，罪必加矣。但清淨安樂，道不失矣。

"Exactly. And so it is with the pursuit of enlightenment. It is only when you find your own pace that enlightenment comes to you. If you try to force things, you end up exhausting yourself. The more exhausted you are, the more doubt grows in your head. And as doubt consumes you, you want nothing but to quit. And if you quit, there goes years of hard work – a waste, a sin. So chill! Take it easy, and enlightenment will be within sight."

佛言：如人鍛鐵，去滓成器，器即精好。學道之人，去心垢染，行即清淨矣。

(35) Impurities of the Mind

Says the Buddha:

When a master forger crafts a weapon, impurities have to be removed from the iron before it is cast into shape. Likewise, as you travel down the path to understanding, the mind needs to be rid of impure thoughts before it can settle into a state of full awareness.

佛言：

　人離惡道，得為人難；

　既得為人，去女即男難；

　既得為男，六根完具難；

　六根既具，生中國難；

　既生中國，值佛世難；

　既值佛世，遇道者難；

　既得遇道，興信心難；

　既興信心，發菩提心難；

既發菩提心，無修無證難。

(36) Count Your Blessings

Says the Buddha:

— Blessed you are to be liberated from hell and born human;
— Born human, thank goodness you are not female but male;
— Male that you are, lucky you are healthy and not deformed;
— Deformity free, fortunate to be born in the civilized world;
— In civilization, how extraordinary to witness the age of revelations;
— Revelations lived, how opportune to have discovered the word;
— The word revealed, how remarkable to have developed faith;
— Faith achieved, only the distinguished foster Bodhi heart;
— Bodhi mastered, exceptional it is to be able to decouple from an attachment to progress and personal achievement.

佛言：佛子離吾數千里，憶念吾戒，
必得道果。在吾左右，雖常見吾，不
順吾戒，終不得道。

(37) Closer to the Truth

Says the Buddha:

Those followers of mine who live in distant corners but observe my teachings to the letter will find the door to enlightenment open. Those who are by my side each day but do not take my lessons to heart will languish in the present state.

佛問沙門：人命在幾間？

對曰：數日間。

佛言：子未知道。復問一沙門：人命在幾間？

對曰：飯食間。

佛言：子未知道。復問一沙門：人命在幾間？

對曰：呼吸間。

佛言：善哉！子知道矣。

(38) Life is Ephemeral

Says the Buddha to his audience of sramanas:
"At what pace do we live this life of ours?"

Answers a sramana:
"We live from day to day."

"You don't get it," answers the Buddha, who turns to another sramana: "At what pace do we live this life of ours?"

Sramana:
"We live from meal to meal."

"That's not it," answers the Buddha, who turns to yet another sramana: "At what pace do we live this life of ours?"

Sramana:
"We live between this breath and the next."

Buddha:
"Well said. May the truth be with you."

佛言：學佛道者，佛所言說，皆應信順。譬如食蜜，中邊皆甜，吾經亦爾。

(39) All the Truth and Nothing but the Truth

Says the Buddha:

All you devoted to my teachings, have faith in every word I say. Imagine how when you taste honey, the all-pervasive sweetness consumes you inside and out. Expect to feel the same when the full force of my truths hits you hard.

佛言：沙門行道，無如磨牛，身雖行道，心道不行。

心道若行，何用行道？

(40) All in Your Heart

Says the Buddha:

Getting you to follow my teachings shouldn't have to be like driving an ox. For if you go through the motions but don't have it in your heart to learn, what use is it?

Then again, if you have it in your heart to pursue the calling, teachings or no teachings, what difference does it make?

佛言：夫為道者，如牛負重，行深泥中，疲極不敢，左右顧視。出離淤泥，乃可蘇息。

沙門當觀情欲甚於淤泥。直心念道，可免苦矣。

(41) Desire Hinders

Says the Buddha:

The journey down the spiritual path is much like that of an ox dragging a heavy load knee-deep in mud. He looks around, desperately searching for a way out, for he knows that only when the mud is cleared is there the possibility of relief.

Sramanas beware: mud can slow you down, but desire even more so, and only those pure at heart and fully committed to the cause will ever find relief from suffering.

佛言：

吾視王候之位如過隙塵，

　視金玉之寶如瓦礫，

　視紈素之服如敝帛，

　視大千界如一訶子，

　視阿耨池水如塗足油，

　視方便門如化寶聚，

　視無上乘如夢金帛，

　視佛道如眼前華，

　視禪定如須彌柱，

　視涅槃如晝夕寤，

　視到正如六龍舞，

　視平等如一真地

　視興化如四時木。

(42) Beyond Illusion

Says the Buddha:

The glory of kings and queens,
  to me is like ashes in the wind,
The splendor of gold and silver,
  for me no better than broken tiles;
Satins and exquisite silks,
  I can scarcely tell apart from tattered rags,
The waters of Lake Anavatapta,
  no holier than the balm I rub on my feet;
The world and its many wonders,
  I find less amusing than a shriveled nut.

Whereas the Supreme Vehicle
  Is my technicolor dreamcoat,
And pathways to fulfillment
  Are the ultimate crown jewels;
Dhyana looms large
  Like Mount Sumeru ahead,
And *nirvana* sobers
  Like awakening from a dream;
The teachings of Buddha
  Dance like flowers before my eyes,
And reality shifts
  Like a consort of a half-dozen slithering serpents;
That we are one and the same
  Is the only true constant,
And so we grow spiritually
  Like a tree moving through the seasons.

諸大比丘，聞佛所說，歡喜奉行。

The consort of Bhiksus were moved by the truths the Buddha imparted, and in wonderment set out to live their lives accordingly.

八大人覺經

後漢沙門安世高譯

Chris Wen-chao Li

Eight Revelations from the Realm of Higher Beings

Translated from the Chinese of Lokottama

為佛弟子，常於晝夜，至心誦念八大人覺：

May each avowed disciple of the Buddha recite these truths daily and nightly, keeping close at heart these eight fundamental understandings of the realm of higher beings –

第一覺悟：世間無常；國土危脆，四
大苦空，五陰無我，生滅變異，虛偽
無主，心是惡源，形為罪藪，如是觀
察，漸離生死。

● THE FIRST UNDERSTANDING being that the world is impermanent, and the earth we tread on is fragile; that inherent in the essences of matter are misery and emptiness, and that mind and matter are devoid of self; that all can change in the blink of an eye through impalpable forces beyond our control; that evil originates in the mind, and sin grows in our flesh – with this understanding, we rise above the cycle of death and rebirth.

第二覺知：多欲為苦；生死疲勞，從
貪欲起，少欲無為，身心自在。

● THE SECOND UNDERSTANDING being that desire is at the root of all suffering; that greed is what binds us to the insufferable cycle of rebirth, and that non-indulgence holds the key to liberating body and mind.

第三覺知：心無厭足，唯得多求，增長罪惡；菩薩不爾，常念知足，安貧守道，唯慧是業。

- THE THIRD UNDERSTANDING being that the need to acquire and the hunger for more adds to our mortal sins, and is a path shunned by those of higher intellect; better to avoid excesses and live the simple but honest life, and allow oneself to accumulate nothing other than wisdom.

第四覺知：懈怠墜落；常行精進，破
煩惱惡，摧伏四魔，出陰界獄。

- THE FOURTH UNDERSTANDING being that idleness leads to ruin, whereas discipline provides the key to banishing illusion, conquering inner demons, and breaking free from the prison of our senses.

第五覺悟：愚癡生死；菩薩常念，廣學多聞，增長智慧，成就辯才，教化一切，悉以大樂。

- THE FIFTH UNDERSTANDING being that with an aim to leading us past the cycle of death and rebirth, manifold beings from higher dimensions have been working to advance their knowledge, perfect their wisdom, and exercise their eloquence so that they may deliver to us the message which will banish our ignorance and transport us to a state of pure bliss.

第六覺知：貧苦多怨，橫結惡緣；菩
薩布施，等念怨親，不念舊惡，不憎
惡人。

- THE SIXTH UNDERSTANDING being that poverty harbors misgivings and adds to the buildup of negativity, for which reason beings of a higher order give aid to the needy, and do so without discrimination as to whether the supplicant is kith or kin, saint or sinner, friend or foe.

第七覺悟：五欲過患；雖為俗人，不染世樂，常念三衣，瓦缽法器，志願出家，守道清白，梵行高遠，慈悲一切。

●   THE SEVENTH UNDERSTANDING being that the five
      senses corrupt our morals, for which reason even
      laymen should refrain from worldly pleasures,
      and be clothed in vestment and habit, ever
      holding in their thoughts the Buddha's teachings
      and acts of charity; those choosing to join the
      order must keep to the straight path and aim to
      broaden their spiritual horizons so as to show
      compassion to all.

第八覺知：生死熾然，苦惱無量；發大乘心，普濟一切，願代眾生，受無量苦，令諸眾生，畢竟大樂。

● THE EIGHTH UNDERSTANDING being that all whose eyes have been opened to the tortuous wheel of death and rebirth shall willingly suffer on behalf of the masses and vow to ferry them to the other shore, so as to deliver salvation and bring joy to all.

如此八事，乃是諸佛，菩薩大人，之所覺悟，精進行道，慈悲修慧，乘法身船，至涅槃岸。復還生死，度脫眾生。

These eight visions form the common currency of spirituality on the order of buddhas, bodhisattvas, and other divine entities, namely, the attainment of wisdom and compassion through moral and spiritual discipline, through which the teachings of our masters shall serve as the vehicle that will transport us to the Realm of Enlightenment, where we will choose not to linger, but instead return to earth after this life to help ferry the masses away from suffering to the blessed shore.

以前八事，開導一切，令諸眾生，覺
生死苦，捨離五欲，修心聖道。

These eight visions shall open the eyes of the huddled masses to the need to navigate away from the wheel of death and rebirth, and to forsake all mortal desire so as to embark on the straight path to spiritual salvation.

若佛弟子，誦此八事，於念念中，滅無量罪，進趣菩提，速登正覺，永斷生死，常住快樂。

Avowed disciples of the Buddha who recite these
truths and keep their lessons close at heart shall be
purged of their manifold sins and put on the
accelerated path to spiritual wisdom, ultimately
attaining omniscient awareness, with which they will
be able to break free from the cycle of mortality and
forever remain in a state of pure bliss.

般若波羅蜜多心經

唐三藏法師玄奘譯

Chris Wen-chao Li

The Heart of the
Virtue of Wisdom

The *Prajñāpāramitā* Heart Sūtra, translated
from the Chinese of Hsüan Tsang

觀自在菩薩，行深般若波羅蜜多時，
照見五蘊皆空，度一切苦厄。

Time was, when the bodhisattva Avalokiteśvara was deeply absorbed in meditation upon the virtue of wisdom[5], it dawned on him that the facets of the self[6] were all illusory – the key, he discovered, through which lies the end of suffering.

---

[5] Sanskrit *prajñāpāramitā,* translated variably as "the virtue of wisdom", "the perfection of wisdom", or "transcendental wisdom".

[6] A reference to the five *skandhas*, namely, (1) the physical realm, (2) the sensual realm, (3) the rational realm, (4) the realm of cognizance, and (5) the realm of consciousness.

舍利子！色不異空，空不異色；色即
是空，空即是色；受想行識，亦復如
是。

Hear this, Shariputra[7], the physical realm is illusory, for illusion necessitates physical semblance. In other words, matter is without substance, and substance is immaterial. The same can be said of the sensual realm, the rational realm, the realm of cognizance, and the realm of consciousness.

---

[7] Shariputra—disciple of the Buddha to which Avalokiteśvara addresses this sermon. Etymologically, the name is derived from Sanskrit *shari-* "bird with large and beautiful eyes" (most likely name of mother) and *–putra* "child" or "son".

舍利子！是諸法空相，不生不滅，不
垢不淨，不增不減。

Shariputra, know that the illusory nature of these mental constructs means that they are false and cannot be produced or destroyed, are never pure or corrupted, and do not multiply or diminish.

是故空中無色，
無受、想、行、識，
無眼、耳、鼻、舌、身、意，
無色、聲、香、味、觸、法；

The physical realm is one such grand illusion, to which we might add the sensual realm, the rational realm, the realm of cognizance, and the realm of consciousness[8].

Likewise the eyes, the ears, the nose, the tongue, the tactile organs, and the mind are all illusory, as are the sense of vision, the sense of hearing, the sense of smell, the sense of taste, the sense of touch, and the sense of reasoning[9].

---

[8] The five *skandhas*, as referred to in the opening line.

[9] The twelve *āyatanas*, or "points of contact with the external world", consisting of the six sensory receptors (1) eyes, (2) ears, (3) nose, (4) tongue, (5) tactile organs, and (6) mind, and the six sensory stimuli (1) visual imagery, (2) sound, (3) smell, (4) taste, (5) touch, and (6) ideas.

無眼界，乃至無意識界；
無無明，亦無無明盡；
乃至無老死，亦無老死盡；

Illusory are the Eighteen Sensory Primes[10], from the eyes all the way to the consciousness of the mind.

Illusory also are the links of the Grand Causal Chain[11]: believe not in ignorance or an end to ignorance; nor is there aging and death or an end to such.

---

[10] The eighteen *dhātus*, consisting of six receptors, six stimuli, and six forms of consciousness – the six receptors being (1) the eyes, (2) the ears, (3) the nose, (4) the tongue, (5) the tactile organs, and (6) the mind; the six stimuli being (1) visual imagery, (2) sound, (3) smell, (4) taste, (5) touch, and (6) ideas; and the six forms of consciousness being (1) visual consciousness, (2) aural consciousness, (3) olfactory consciousness, (4) gustatory consciousness, (5) tactile consciousness, and (6) mental consciousness

[11] The twelve *nidānas*, also known as the "twelve causal links" or the "twelve links in the chain of dependent origination", namely:

- from (1) ignorance arises (2) delusion;
- from (2) delusion arises (3) consciousness
- from (3) consciousness arises (4) individual identity;
- from (4) individual identity arises (5) the physical senses;
- from (5) physical senses arise (6) sensory interaction;
- from (6) sensory interaction arises (7) sensuality;
- from (7) sensuality arises (8) craving;
- from (8) craving arises (9) attachment;
- from (9) attachment arises (10) sense of being;
- from (10) sense of being arises (11) physical birth;
- from (11) physical birth arises (12) aging and death

無苦、集、滅、道，
無智亦無得。

Similarly without base are the Four Noble Truths[12], for there is no suffering or a cause for suffering, nor is there an end to suffering or an awakening that brings about such an end. No such liberating knowledge exists, so perish the thought of ever achieving such a state.

---

[12] The four noble truths being (1) that life consists of suffering, (2) that suffering is brought about by desire; (3) that an end to suffering is within reach, and (4) that the path to ending suffering lies with achieving full mindfulness.

以無所得故，菩提薩埵，依般若波羅
蜜多故，心無罣礙；

無罣礙故，無有恐怖，遠離一切顛倒
夢想，究竟涅槃。

And because the mind is not intent on achieving, bodhisattvas who abide by the virtue of wisdom are burdened with no emotional baggage.

Without baggage, they are able to see delusions for what they are and inch ever closer to a state of bliss[13].

[13] Sanskrit *nirvāṇa* — "end to suffering"; "state of pure bliss".

~ 137 ~

三世諸佛，依般若波羅蜜多故，得阿
耨多羅三藐三菩提。

Know that it is through the virtue of wisdom that buddhas of past, present and future realms reach enlightenment of the highest order[14] —

---

[14] Sanskrit *anuttarā samyak-saṃbodhi*, literally "unexcelled supreme enlightenment".

故知般若波羅蜜多，是大神咒，是大
明咒，是無上咒，是無等等咒，能除
一切苦，真實不虛。

for which reason we believe the virtue of wisdom to
be a doctrine unique and unrivaled in every way,
a mantra so fine, so radiant, so divine —
an end to all grief, bringing truest relief!

故說般若波羅蜜多咒，即說咒曰：

揭諦揭諦，
波羅揭諦，
波羅僧揭諦，
菩提薩婆訶。

So recite the mantra of the virtue of wisdom,
and do so in this way:

> *Go forth, go forth —*
> *Go forth past the pearly gates,*
> *Where enlightenment awaits*[15].

---

[15] Cultural paraphrase of Sanskrit *gate gate pāragate pārasaṃgate bodhi svāhā*.

Printed in Great Britain
by Amazon

38411904R00098